Table of Contents

I. Why Email Marketing 4
II. Marketing Prework: You Should Have Done This First 8
III. What are the Laws? 12
IV. Build Your List 18
V. What Makes a Good Email? 24
VI. Email Message 29
VII. Create Your Email Campaign 35
VIII. Types of Campaigns 40
IX. Sample Campaigns 47
X. Get Your Emails in the Inbox 53
XI. Get Your Emails Opened 61
XII. Get the Clicks 67
XIII. Get Conversions 77
XIV. What to Measure 82
XV. Conclusion 86
XVI. Tips from Email Marketing Professionals 88
APPENDIX 1 Definitions 95
APPENDIX 2 Real Life Examples 99
APPENDIX 3 The Buyer's Journey in Detail 125

Introduction

My email marketing and marketing automation career started when I was responsible for business development and revenue generation.

You see, I was good at building relationships. But when it came to closing sales, I was mediocre (at best). And I wanted to be a top performer.

I had always loved marketing and sales. So, I dug deeper into ways to help me generate more leads and nurture my existing leads.

I wanted to create a system that pulled more people into my sales pipeline and that moved them through the sales stages to become buyers.

My company constantly asked for forecasting numbers, and I never thought it was valuable. I had no idea who was going to drop into my quarter for sales.

I had 1400 companies that were in my area that I saw as clients. While most salespeople chase after larger prospects, I always felt like the smaller companies were willing to pay for a better service and weren't as concerned with squeezing margins.

But chasing after 1000 small companies was near impossible.

That's when I discovered email.

I created a database of all the companies. I visited companies in-person and called them. I then followed up with them using both an email series as well as regular mail.

I automated every piece. I created lead magnets. I researched and wrote white papers, eBooks, and case studies specific for my target market.

I marketed the hell out of everything I could.

And even with mediocre sales ability, I started to rank in the top 5 every year for my company (out of 1800+ offices).

I didn't market for advertising awards.

I didn't market to have pretty stuff.

I marketed to get the most return on investment. I marketed to get the most return on my time.

And email did it for me. To say that I fell in love with email marketing is an understatement.

Now that I have focused my career on email marketing and marketing automation for the last 6 years, my techniques and strategies have changed. I use more advance tools. I get the help of copywriters, designers, and more.

But my focus has always been and will always be on the return of investment of the campaigns.

And that's why I wrote this book. I wanted to share how email can make all your sales and all your marketing more effective.

If this mediocre salesperson can use email marketing to get more sales and more revenue, you can too!

I. Why Email Marketing

Why should we care about email marketing?

It's effective and has the *highest ROI* of any marketing tactic. That's the most important reason why you should use email marketing. Depending on what study you read, email marketing has a **ROI** (return on investment) of $38-$46 for every $1 spent.

Email is also easy to get started. You can start with a low-priced tool and scale up. You don't need a huge investment to start. Businesses of all sizes and all budgets can implement email marketing.

Email is flexible. You can use email for prospects in all stages of the buyer's journey. You create an email campaign for people that have just determined they have a problem, one for people that are actively looking for a solution, and still another one for recent buyers or clients.

Email allows you to target specific people. Unlike radio, TV, or other media, with email you can target as specific as you want (and as specific as your database allows). For example, you may target women between 30 and 40, that are Director level and above, and that live in Texas. As long as your email program and database allow you to segment (and you have all the data), you can do it.

You own your email list. Unlike social media, you own your list. No one is going to say, "Before you could reach 100% of your people, but now you can only access 7%." With email, you own it, and you make the rules.

Email marketing is easy to measure. With email marketing, you can quickly measure progress and ROI. You can also see that Betty Sue, the Director of Operations of XYZ company, has opened your email, clicked on the call to action and downloaded your eBook, "7 Questions to Ask Materials Suppliers."

Email marketing integrates well with many different types of marketing. Email makes all your other marketing more effective and increases overall conversion. An example: You run a PPC (pay per click) program on Google Ads. You could send each ad to the same or different landing pages. When they go to the page, you grab their email. That way, you keep in touch with them even if they don't buy.

Example:
Magazine Ad - $500
Traffic to site: 500
Converted/Purchased: 5
Leads: 120
Cost to Acquire a Customer: $100 ($500/5 customers)

Google Ads - $500
Traffic to site: 1000
Converted/Purchased: 10
Leads: 350
Cost to Acquire a Customer: $50 ($500/10 customers)

Average cost to acquire a customer is approximately $67 ($1,000/15 customers).

What if we converted just 1% of all leads over the next year?

With 120 leads from the magazine and 350 leads from Google Ads, we have a total of 470 leads. With 1%, we convert 4 more customers.

The new cost to acquire a customer ($1,000/19 customers) is approximately $53.

This is just one example how to make your marketing more effective. Just remember every marketing activity you do, you generate leads in addition to sales. If you can put those leads into a follow up system or funnel (and convert even a very small amount), your marketing conversions will increase and the cost to acquire a client will decrease.

Later in the book we are going to talk about different types of campaigns that are effective. One of these campaigns, the abandoned cart campaign, can increase conversion and increase your revenue per customer dramatically!

Email has an ROI of $38-$46 for every $1 invested

II. Marketing Prework: You Should Have Done This First

Email marketing is AMAZINGGG. Hopefully, you got that message from my first chapter.

However, this book is assuming that you have completed the necessary marketing prework to make all your marketing (including email) more effective.

I'll review a few key things to do for your pre-work.

What is Your Product or Service

Obviously, you know what your product or service is. But can you communicate it easily? You should be able to answer the following:

- What problems does your product or service solve?
- Why should someone buy from you instead of from your competitors or instead of doing nothing?
- What feeling or emotion does your product or service help or fulfill?

Example:
ABC Dry Cleaning
We obviously know what dry cleaning is, but what does it accomplish?

- → We help busy professionals look and feel their best and help them save time with our overnight delivery service.
- → People should buy from us because we provide personalized service, pick up and deliver to any location within 20 miles, include shoe-shine services for free with our dry-cleaning service, and have a frequent buyer program.
- → We provide a feeling of relief for our busy professionals.

Ideal Client

Your ideal client is someone that you have identified as someone that is a perfect fit for your company. One great way to determine your ideal client is to look at your top 10 most profitable clients (don't just look at revenue). Because I have a no asshole rule for clients, I also look at who I love working with.

This doesn't mean it's your only client.

Let's say our ideal client for our dry-cleaning example above is:
- A 30-55 year-old male
- Works in a professional capacity
- Wears dress shirts and slacks daily
- Makes over $100,000 per year
- Travels a certain amount for work every month
- Lives within 20 miles

You created this ideal client persona after looking at your top 10 most profitable clients. These attributes were present in almost all profitable clients. And when you looked at your entire database, clients with these attributes represented more than 80% of your total profit in the previous year.

Your goal with setting your ideal client is to get the most profitable clients (think about cloning your top 10 clients). This doesn't mean that you will turn down a 27-year-old woman that wants her suit cleaned. It just means that typically women of that particular age do not consistently use dry cleaning service and don't use the high profit services.

Note: Most businesses have several 'personas' that they target. You should create a persona for each target client. These will help you when you are running your campaigns. Once you have your ideal client or clients, you should be able to answer these questions:

- What are their biggest problems?
- What are their biggest concerns?
- What keeps them up at night?
- Where do they congregate (both online and offline)?

Do your prework so you're not wasting dollars on the wrong market or the wrong message. Get it right and increase your ROI.

more ideal clients

- *rehom*
- *Stable*
- *BCP council*
- *Bournemouth pier*

III. What are the Laws?

What are the laws for email marketing and data management? There are many laws out there. The three main ones to keep in mind are CAN-SPAM (US), CASL (Canada) and GDPR (European Union).

- CAN-SPAM – Controlling the Assault of Non-Solicited Pornography and Marketing Act of 2003
- CASL – Canada's Anti-Spam Law
- GDPR – General Data Protection Regulation

For all areas, you can send transactional emails. What does that mean? If you go to a website and request a whitepaper, the company can send that whitepaper to you. However, they may not be able to send additional emails unless you explicitly agreed to receive future emails. This additional agreement is often added as a tick box on a website that says that you agree to receive future emails.

Something to keep in mind as you are reading these laws is that you absolutely need to differentiate your list by country. To be safe, I recommend you keeping all non-US countries in a separate list.

CAN-SPAM

You have probably heard of the CAN-SPAM act (or at least heard the word 'spam').

The CAN-SPAM Act of 2003 - Controlling the Assault of Non-Solicited Pornography and Marketing - protects consumers from unsolicited emails.

CAN-SPAM compliance is for the United States. Other countries and areas have some version of CAN-SPAM with similar laws but with a few differences.

To be CAN-SPAM compliant, emails must have the following:
* an obvious unsubscribe link
* truthful subject line
* truthful from address
* street address of the business within the email
* warning for adult content (if applicable)

In addition, CAN-SPAM states that emails must be obtained through a 'legitimate means."

Unsubscribes must be honored within 10 days.
The unsubscribe link needs to be easily identified in the email. Most email providers and email senders have an unsubscribe link at the bottom of the email (often as an anchor text of 'unsubscribe' with a hyperlink). You can offer subscription management that allows the recipient the ability to change the subscriptions (opt into certain email series or a certain frequency).

The from email and name as well as the subject line need to truthfully represent the business and email content. This doesn't mean you cannot get creative. You just need to not be deceitful. For example, you can use from Bob in Sales, Bob, Sales, Customer Service, etc. But you can't say from 'PayPal' if you're not PayPal. For the subject line, again you can be creative. You can say 'Did you see this?' 'You won't believe this…,' 'Here's something you will thank us for later…,' and more. But you can't say 'Here's your Bank of America payment' unless you are Bank of America talking about a payment. ☺

The business mailing address must be included. This can be a street address, a registered PO Box, or a private mailbox. This is sometimes difficult for home-based companies. You can either use your home address or pay for a PO Box or personal mailbox.

Adult content has to come with a warning. This doesn't affect most people reading this. But this is obviously a problem (especially since the 'P' in CAN-SPAM is pornography).

The statement about how the email was obtained for US CAN-SPAM is ambiguous at best. You are allowed to purchase opt in leads if recipients gave permission. Most email service providers forbid purchased lists to be uploaded because of potential issues with being blacklisted for SPAM complaints.

CASL
Canada's email, data and privacy law is more restrictive than the US. In the US, you don't need explicit permission to email. You just need a business case (and need to follow the rules mentioned above).

For Canada, someone needs to explicitly opt in prior to getting an email. Whereas CAN-SPAM assumes consent until the recipient revokes it.
You must also have all of the other requirements than CAN-SPAM has for information, subject, unsubscribe, etc.

GDPR

GDPR was released and has started to be enforced within the past year. GDPR is a comprehensive data and privacy law that also covers email.

GDPR takes a very conservative stance on emails. Similar to Canada, GDPR requires explicit opt-in. GDPR also has additional requirements when it comes to data and privacy. People can request that their information be 'forgotten' and completely removed.

GDPR also differentiates between countries. Some countries require a single opt-in and others (like the Netherlands) require a double opt-in.

What does double opt-in mean? Let's say someone from the Netherlands went to the website and signed up to receive newsletters and other communications from a country. Since the Netherlands is a double opt-in country, there's a trigger that sends them another email to 'confirm their opt in.' This person is not considered marketable until they click to confirm their opt in (even though they requested the communication).

GDPR packs a HEFTY penalty if you do not comply. There are different tiers, but the penalty could be 4% of global revenue or 20 million pounds ($27 million+ --- yikes!).
GDPR is evolving. To make sure you are compliant, go to https://gdpr.eu.

It's important to research and review all applicable laws prior to creating any type of campaign. If you are marketing to an international database, it's VERY important to look at each country's laws.

Maxing out your ROI is about increasing revenue (high R) AND decreasing expenses (low I). Avoid undue costs like fines.

IV. Build Your List

"The money is in the list." If you've read any marketing book in the last 10 years, you will have undoubtedly come across this saying or quote.

It's not a lie. If you have an engaged, responsive list that is a good size (doesn't have to be huge but the bigger the better if it's responsive), you will make money.

But how do you build your list?

You can use many ways to build your list.

We are going to talk about building your opt-in list. However, for business to business (B2B), there are many companies that successfully use cold lists to build relationships with and stay in front of a targeted market. I will touch on a way to use a cold list to build a warm, engaged list. As mentioned in the previous chapter, you should make sure your marketing automation platform or email service provider allows for purchasing leads prior to paying any money.

Cold Emails to Build a Warm List

Many email marketing professionals are dead set against cold emails (and many ESPs or email service providers don't allow it). I understand why because so many companies do a terrible job of segmenting their list, identifying the real concerns of their target market, and just blast BS instead of providing value.

I see cold emails as a great way to quickly sift through a targeted list.

Why do I say targeted? Because if you go to a good list provider, you can drill down and get a very specific list. For example, you can get women over the age of 45, that are directors or higher at a SAAS (software as a service) company, and that are decision makers for CRM (customer relationship management) software. If you know your ideal client, you can quickly find a list of highly qualified decision makers.

You can create a short email series with a very targeted message that speaks to these people and provides tons of value (not a series of sales pitches). You want these people to think "this email was super helpful" even if they never buy from you.

Use the engagement as your filter. If the recipient opens and engages, move them to a warm list. If they don't, put this list aside and try to warm them up again in 6 months.

With this warm list, put them into a beautiful nurture campaign to help answer questions, provide value, and build trust. I talk about nurture campaigns later in the book.

Ads

Use online and offline ads to push people to a landing page that captures their contact information. You can either give away something (eBook, white paper, etc.) or you can sell something that is a low-price offer (often called a trip wire).

If you give away something, you will get a higher number of leads. But if you sell something, you now have a list of buyers. And buyers that buy $7 items also buy $20k items. A buyer's list is more valuable. But it just depends on the goal of your campaign.

Examples of online ads include Google AdWords, social media ads, ads on other blogs, promotions on other social media pages, etc. Examples of offline ads include TV, radio, billboards, magazines, newspapers, newsletters, etc.

For ads, it's important you have a specific landing page for each ad. One of the worst things you can do is create an ad then push them to your home page on your website. You want it to be easy for the prospect or visitor to know exactly what they need to do (so make sure that call to action is clear).

Something that you need to do *before* you create any ads is identify your target market. You will be building an audience (specifically for online ads). You will also want to know exactly what your ideal audience wants and needs, what concerns they have, and what questions they need answered.

Social Media
We mentioned social media advertising above. But this section is specifically for organic only (no paid ads).
You will follow a similar plan as above. You will need an offer, and you'll be pushing people to a lead magnet (freebie) or a special low-price offer.

Offline Networking

Many businesspeople are involved in networking groups. But they really miss the biggest benefit of going to these events. You can add people to a networking list and follow #1 (cold emails). You can also promote your freebie or offer and incent your warm network to go to your landing page and sign up for it.

You can ask your network to share your emails or share your posts. This is an easy way for your network to help you.

MOST IMPORTANT NETWORKING TIP: Make sure to provide value to people, to refer to people, and to help people. If you choose to GIVE FIRST, your network will see you as a welcome guest (not a pest) when they receive your emails or requests.

Direct Mail

Direct mail is not used as often but is still effective. Direct mail can be used to sell directly and to build your list.
Similar to the approach of ads, you will want to get a list of people that are your target market and push them to a landing page (push them from offline to online). This landing page can sell a low-priced item or service or give away a freebie.

Other Marketing

Anything that you do to sell can be used to build your list. By integrating your email into all your marketing activities, you can make your marketing more effective and build a BIG, BEAUTIFUL LIST!

**Your email marketing list is gold.
It doesn't have to be huge to have
a high ROI.
An engaged list = $$**

V. What Makes a Good Email?

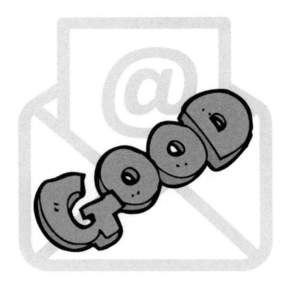

When creating an email, you should start with the best practices for email marketing for your industry. Once you have a decent volume of emails and list, you should test every component of your email. While best practices are great, your database may be very different. By testing, you can optimize every part of your marketing and increase your overall effectiveness.

From Email / Address
Typically, a person's name works better than a company name or department. The same goes for the email address. Bonus tip: If the person's name you are using is recognizable (i.e. it's the Customer Success Manager they are used to talking to or it's a well known CEO), your open rate increases.

Subject Line
Personalization works. Everyone loves to see their name and their company name. It's crazy. We all know that you can personalize emails automatically. But IT STILL WORKS at making emails more effective.

Other subject line best practices include using numbers and statistics, asking questions, and relating your email to something that has been in recent news.

Here's a resource page for this book. Check out the list of subject lines that have worked.

http://robynhatfield.com/email-resources

For do => we can turn our blogs in to newsletter

Preview Text

Preview text is an often forgotten, overlooked, and ignored marketing tool that is GOLDEN. The preview text is the text that shows up under the subject line in someone's inbox.

In many email providers, the preview text is a separate section or widget. If you don't include something in your preview text, your email service provider may leave it blank or may add the first few sentences of the email.

Email Body

Usually, shorter emails perform better than longer emails. This isn't always true because some audiences like more detail (a great example is engineers).

The messaging and the content need to be TARGETED to the specific audience. Most people do a TERRIBLE job at this (even experienced marketers). Don't sell. Provide value. Answer questions. If you want people to take an action, you should focus on what's important to them. Then give them a very clear call to action to take. I go into more detail in the next chapter on messaging.

The email needs to look clean. The HTML needs to be clean (or some email service providers will push it to junk).

I have seen a better response from emails with no images. But this is one you will want to test. If you have a product that needs to be shown, it probably makes sense to have some high-quality images.

call to action button in red

For the call to action, buttons typically work better than links. You will want to have 1 call to action repeated several times in the email. I would suggest a call to action at the top of the email and at the bottom. You may want to include a link somewhere in the middle.

The color of the button is also important. I have seen a 120% increase in clicks just by changing the button color. I would test this. In general, red has worked better for me. But test the color.

Test the call to action on the button. For the words on the button, use very few words. It's better to start with an action word. Example, "Download This Report" or "Watch This Video".

Email Signature

While it may be an afterthought for most people, the email signature can be very effective if used properly. Most people just have their company logo, name, and contact information (and if the email is a bulk email with no name, even worse).

Use the signature space. If you are sending from a person (vs. sending from a department or sending from the company in general), use their personal signature as well as put a clickable banner or clickable link in the signature. Do you have an event coming up you want to promote? Is there some collateral that is relevant to your email? Or maybe just use it for your main CTA (in addition to the other areas).

> **By optimizing every component of your email, you can increase conversion and ROI 100%+! An engaged list = $$**

VI. Email Message

Email messaging is so important that it deserves its own chapter.

Most people get this wrong. They get this REALLY, REALLY WRONG.

So how do you get it right?

Start with Your Ideal Client

You better have a darn good idea who your ideal client is before starting. This has to be first! Everyone talks about an ideal client, but few companies really take the time and effort needed to make this crystal clear.

If you are B2B, you show know (at a minimum):
- Size of company (both in terms of employees and revenue $$)
- Industry and sub-industry
- Geo-location
- Stage of company (start up, established, mature)

If you are B2C or B2B (because you sell to a person not a business), you should know:
- Male or Female
- Age
- Income
- Job Title
- Job Function / Level
- Major concerns, problems, and pain points
- Where do they gather (online and offline)

Questions You Should Answer About Your Ideal Client

A great way to prepare for your campaigns is to get all your content together. By answering these questions below, you will have a better idea of what to include (and what not to include) in your email campaign.

- What are 3-5 problems/concerns for this person as it pertains to your product or service?
- What are 3-5 obstacles they are facing as it pertains to your product or service?
- What are the possible solutions to the above problems (could be a direct competitor or could be some type of workaround)?
- What are the most common objections for buying your product or service?
- What are reasons not to buy your product or service?
- What are the key things happening in your industry right now that pertain to your product or service?
- What are buzzworthy happenings or cool key benefits people look for in your industry as it pertains to your product or service?

Create Some Collateral

You need some collateral. You need 'good stuff' to send people to.

What do I mean by collateral?

You should create articles, blogs, eBooks, booklets, videos, audios, podcasts, whitepapers, webinars and more.
Your website should be full of this beautiful stuff. You should have some gated and ungated. Gated means you have to

complete a form to get the asset. Non-gated means you can access it without filling out a form.

You need to have questions answered as well as collateral that goes into detail giving detailed answers and steps to help your ideal client.

Create Emails

Now that you've answered the questions and created the collateral, it's time to start writing those emails.

You will want to go through each question and create emails that go with each one.

For example, you answer the 3-5 problems. You will want to write an email for EACH of the 5 problems:

- Is this a problem you're having? You're going to explain that other people have said this was a common problem.
- Problem details…Explain exactly what the problem is. This not only helps them understand the problem, but it also shows that YOU understand their problems.
- Do you suffer from… You're not just talking about the problem, but what the problem causes. Talk about the real PAIN of the problem.

Here's an example:
"Is workplace safety and worker's compensation a concern for you?
We often hear from our clients in the manufacturing industry that one of the things that keeps them up at night is workplace safety.

As the Plant Manager, we know that you are not only responsible for workplace safety, but we also know that you are responsible for the P&Ls of your plant. With worker's compensation being a huge expense that significantly decreases overall profitability, we know that you keep a sharp eye on this.

We wrote a blog about ways to increase workplace safety and reducing accidents. You can also download our workplace safety checklist that has been used by companies like yours to reduce accidents by over 60%.

Read the Blog

Create Your Sequences and Campaigns

After you create all your emails based on the questions and collateral, you now will want to lay out a sequence. There are different ways to create campaigns. Those campaigns can be long term nurtures or short-term campaigns.

The biggest driver of what type of campaign to use is your goals. If you are warming up a cold list, you may go with a short email sequence or campaign. If you have a warm list, you may decide to create a long-term nurture program that walks people through the buyer's journey.

In the next chapter will talk a little bit more about campaigns and touch on different styles later in the book.

Messaging is key to getting opens, clicks, and _conversions_.

Don't skimp on messaging.

VII. Create Your Email Campaign

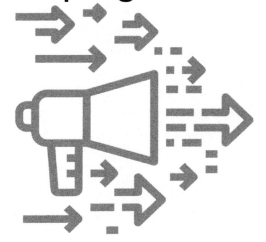

Email marketing needs to be both strategically and tactically planned and executed.

Audience
You should know your audience. I know I've mentioned this several times throughout the book. But EVERY time you create ANY marketing, you should have your ideal client or target market in mind.

By the time you start creating campaigns, you already have your ideal client. You may need to segment your database or narrow it.

For example, your product may be beneficial across many industries. But for this campaign, you are specifically going after manufacturing industries. Your campaign is going to be written for someone making decisions about contingent staffing for your company. You will want to segment your database by industry and filter your list by job title or function.

Goals
What is the goal of the campaign? Seems like a silly question to ask. But most marketers don't answer this question before they start creating their content and before they create their campaigns.

Questions to ask:
- What is the goal?
- What does success look like?
- How will we measure success?

Content

You've already created the content. You know what questions you have. You know what collateral you can use. Now it's time to write those sequences and write those messages with your specific audience in mind.

In the example we used before, you will be tailoring a very specific message to people that hire contingent workers for manufacturing companies. It's important that you keep this specific person in mind. What he/she is concerned with is very different than what the CEO, CFO, or accounting manager would be concerned with.

It's important to think of emails as conversations. You know who you are talking to. How would you talk to this person? Write it like that! For example, if we had 2 different campaigns with one focused on the Director of Operations and one focused on the hiring managers, you would use different language and different pain points.

Most people get this wrong! They send the same email to every contact at a company. They talk to very different people the same way. And that's one of the many reasons why their emails suck!

Make sure to use the language that these specific people use. You can create credibility and trust by using the jargon or terminology used by your targeted campaign audience.

Create the Email Flow

Now you have your content, messaging, and collateral to link to. Let's create the flow in a series.

This flow will depend on what type of campaign you use.

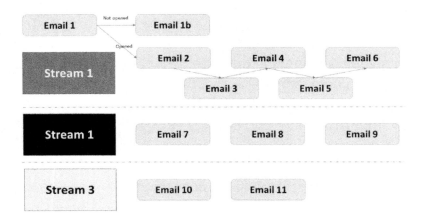

Email 1 is sent. If it's not opened, email 1b is sent (which is almost identical to email 1 except the subject line is changed).

If email 1 or 1b is opened, we send email 2. We then send email 3, 4, 5, and 6 with a 2-week cadence (2 weeks in between each email).

If the recipient opens and clicks on 3 key links in the links in the first stream, they get moved to the 2nd stream. They could receive all emails or only a few depending on their actions.

Stream 2 begins, and the recipient starts to receive the emails 1 week apart (emails 7, 8, and 9). Stream 2 is ONLY people that have engaged (and were then moved to stream 2).

Stream 3 is kicked off if a recipient in stream 2 opens and clicks on 2 keys links. Stream 3 is ONLY people that have engaged (and were then moved to stream 3). Stream 3 has email 10 and 11 and are sent 3 days apart.

This example is a triggered email campaign that is designed to provide content more quickly for people that are hyper-engaged. And for people that don't engage, they are shut off after email 6 (and only receive an email every 2 weeks).

Create your flow.
Create your emails.
And create ROI magic!

VIII. Types of Campaigns

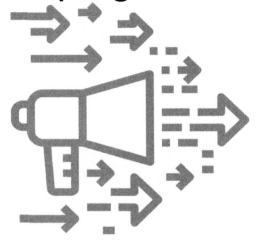

⊗ Sea Sim launch campaign

Your goals will determine the type of campaigns you run. You most likely will have several different types of campaigns that are running at any given time in your organization.

Type of campaigns we will discuss are:
- One-off email sends
- Event series
- Drip campaign – date driven
- Drip campaign – trigger driven
- Nurture campaign

One-Off Email Send
I am generally not a fan of the one-off email send. However, there are some uses for this type of email. A few examples of this are more transactional in nature.

- Announcement of an outage in a product or a store closing
- A quick announcement that wasn't anticipated (a product that is going on sale that wasn't anticipated)
- Any other transactional email. An example of a transactional email is someone signing up for content or collateral on your website and the email is sent to deliver the product (i.e. someone signed up for an eBook, and this program automatically delivers it).

Event Series
If you are hosting an event or participating in an event, event series are different than other email campaigns.
Series are helpful to use for user conferences, tradeshows that you are participating in, webinars, and more.

An example of a series of emails for a webinar may be:
- Invite 1 – Goes out to your targeted list and notifies them of an upcoming webinar that is 3 weeks away.
- Invite 2 – Notifies any person that has not registered for the webinar. This is sent 2 weeks before the event.
- Invite 3 – Notifies any person that has not registered for the webinar. This is sent 1 week before the event.
- Invite 4 – Notifies any person that has not registered for the webinar. This is sent 1 day before the event.
- Triggered confirmation email – Confirmation is sent immediately to anyone that signed up for the event. This will have all the key information such as how to sign into the webinar, what you need to do prior to the event (example – test your system to make sure it will work), and a calendar invite that saves the date on their calendar program (ex. Outlook Calendar invite).
- Reminder confirmation email – Confirmation email is sent again 1 day prior to the event and has all the information in the triggered confirmation email.
- Reminder 1 hour before the event – Short email that is just a reminder saying, "Sign into our webinar in an hour."

Drip Campaign – Date Driven
A drip campaign is a series of emails that are sent to a list/prospect. They call it 'drip' because the emails are 'dripped' into the inbox.
For the date driven one, we usually see a series that is set at a specific cadence. For example, we send it every 14 days.

You can also set the emails to send on specific days.
Example: Email 1 goes out on the 1st, email 2 goes out on the

12th, email 3 goes out on the 19th, and email 4 goes out on the 15th.

People often get drip campaigns confused with nurtures. A drip campaign sends all emails no matter what the recipient does. Most simple email service providers have this functionality.

Drip campaigns are not as effective as other campaigns because they don't take into consideration the level of engagement of the prospect.

<u>Drip Campaign – Trigger Driven</u>
While this is still a drip campaign, we use triggers that drive the send dates. While this is still not a nurture campaign, it is typically more effective than a date driven drip campaign.

Why?

It takes into consideration the engagement of the audience. The campaign can also be evergreen. This means you can leave it 'turned on' to pull people into the campaign or run the campaign constantly.

An example of a drip campaign that is trigger driven:
Email 1 is sent. If email 1 is not opened, email 1b is sent in 3 days. When email 1 or 1b is opened, email 2 is sent 7 days later. If email 1 or 1b is not opened, there are no other emails sent.

**An important point to remember is that both trigger-driven and date-driven drip campaigns can have a trigger at the

beginning. Once the campaign is started, then the emails can then be triggered or be pushed by date.

Trigger at beginning – Series starts when someone requests something on the website.

Pushed email – Email 1 starts when we set the date and push it out.

Nurture Campaign

Nurture campaigns are the most comprehensive email programs that companies typically have. EVERY company should have some type of nurture in place.

A nurture program typically flows along with the buyer's journey. I go into more detail about the buyer's journey later in the book. But a quick explanation is that the buyer's journey is the path the buyer goes through as they go from prospect to customer. In many buyer's journeys you have the Awareness stage, Consideration stage, and the Decision stage. After the Decision stage, it usually makes sense to have an onboarding drip series as well as a retention focused series.

| Awareness | Consideration | Decision |

Nurture campaigns are all about triggers. Similar to the drip campaign, the series has streams or sections for each stage of the journey. To move to the next stream or section, the recipient of the email has to take specific actions.

One key difference in nurtures and drip campaigns is that nurtures should be evergreen. Drip campaigns are usually started at a specific time. Nurtures usually 'pull' people into the campaign based on specific parameters or criteria.

Example: You have a program that as soon as someone is created in the database that meets specific criteria (ex. they are engineering managers in the chemical engineering industry), they are added to a specific nurture campaign. Or you can say that as someone is a 'success' in another program (ex. they attend a webinar, they open a drip campaign series, they download a book), they are added to a specific nurture.

You can structure nurture programs many different ways. You can make different nurture programs for different stages. Or you can create an all-encompassing nurture that has many streams with many emails within those streams.

A few different streams you will want to account for include:
1) New prospects
2) New HOT prospects (people that are new but filled out a high-intent form like a demo request or meeting request)
3) Recycle to marketing (when the sales team contacts the lead, but they are not ready to buy --- so we push them back to marketing to get nurtured and warmed up)
4) Closed lost (when a contact or lead had an active opportunity, but we lost them to the competition)
5) Closed abandoned (when a contact or lead had an active opportunity, but they just went dark on us)

Nurture campaigns should be a beautiful example of the buyer's journey. When done correctly, you will create a steady stream of qualified buyers by providing people in your database the information they need. When automated, you will help the sales team by consistently giving them qualified leads on a regular basis. If you are your sales team, this will make your sales life SO MUCH BETTER!

Pick the right campaign for the job.

Increase engagement.

Increase ROI

IX. Sample Campaigns

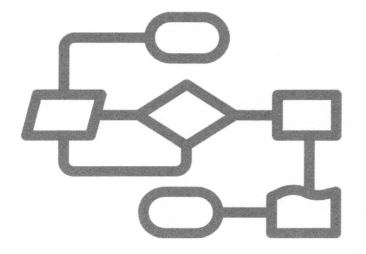

We talked about the types of campaigns earlier in the book. In this chapter I just want to review a few sample campaigns for ideas on how to use different campaigns for different goals and functions.

Cart Abandonment

You are probably all too familiar with the cart abandonment email series because you have received these.

This is when you go to a website, look around, go to buy something (and fill out all the information), then don't buy. You've done everything but provide your payment information.

This is one of the most profitable email sequences or drip campaigns to put in place.

Why?

High content = high conversion. And high conversion = big $$!

Cart abandon emails usually start with something like "Did you forget something?" in the subject line.

The first email should be triggered to send shortly after the cart is abandoned. It should contain information such as:
- Catchy subject line
- Introduction text (use the prospect's name if you have it)
- Items left in the cart (We noticed you left xxx in the cart.)
- Give the offer or discount
- Checkout button or some type of call to action

- Reviews for your product or some type of testimonial
- Closing text

Emails 2 and 3 will be similar. You may choose to wait to offer a discount until email 3.

This campaign would be set up as a time specified campaign.
Email 1 is triggered.
Email 2 is sent 2 days after email 1.
Email 3 is sent 2 days after email 2.

You should add a pause step if the person goes back to the cart and purchases.

Welcome

Welcome emails are very important to send right after someone joins something. It's a great way to warm up the prospect, build rapport, and establish expectations.

Welcome emails are one of the highest opened and clicked emails.

Depending on what people signed up for, you may choose to have a short welcome series campaign. You may also add the welcome email to the front of the nurture program.

Re-engagement Program
Re-engagement programs do exactly what you expect. They re-engage people.

For example, let's say you have a contact that was active at one time. But in the last 12 months, they have not engaged. Before you decide to delete them from your database (to maintain good data hygiene), you do one last ditch effort to get them engaged.

Re-engagement programs can be a stream in the nurture series (similar to a closed abandoned or a recycle to marketing). They can also be a stand-alone drip campaign.

A few key things to keep in mind for re-engagement series:
- Make your message clear. Make sure it's clear that you are looking to engage with them. Keep the message short, concise, and to the point.
- Make it personalized. Your database and email service provider should make this easy. Use their name. If applicable use their company and other information you have in your database (that you can pull in with tokens or other personalization features of your ESP).
- Include link triggers to stay on the list or be removed. Make it easy for them to stay on the list or opt out. If they don't ask to stay on, you should remove them (think about your overall deliverability on this one).
- Emails 2 and 3 are reiterating what the first one did. You are going to follow all the above rules but just change it up.

Comeback Campaign

This series is specifically for lost customers. Unlike the re-engagement, we are talking about more than people not interacting with your email. You lost $$ because you lost their business.

Usually, you lose business and don't ever hear anything. Most people hate bad reviews, but with bad reviews at least you know why someone left.

For most unsatisfied customers, they just stop buying. Think about the last time you went to a hair stylist, a chiropractor, a dentist or some other professional that you weren't happy with. Did you just stop going? I know I am guilty of this.

The comeback campaign can be crazy profitable if you do it right.

Email 1 is acknowledgement that you haven't seen them around. For a chiropractor, you may say "We've noticed you haven't set an appointment in a while. We hope it wasn't something we did. We would love to see you again. If you click the link below, you can schedule an appointment with us right away."

Email 2 is the incentive. You're going to do something similar to the above about acknowledging you haven't seen them in a while. But you are going to give an incentive. An example could be 25% off the next visit or get our free fitness and agility assessment value at $99 for free at your next visit.

Email 3 is a reminder of the offer.

Email 4 is a goodbye.

**Important note: If you did something wrong or upset them, you may want to use a one-to-one personalized email or call.

> **The global cart abandonment is 75.6%. Imaging recapturing just a portion of that in a campaign!**

X. Get Your Emails in the Inbox

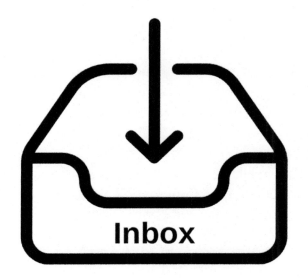

You may have written the most amazing emails in the world. But if your emails don't arrive in the inbox, it doesn't matter! When we talk about getting in the inbox, we are talking about email deliverability.

What is email deliverability?

Email deliverability is measured by taking the total number of emails delivered divided by the total number of emails sent. You are looking for the highest number possible (with as close to 100% as possible).

Email deliverability is HUGE. Getting deliverability right takes a combination of setting up the right technical pieces, following good data hygiene practices, and keeping with email best practices.

Data Hygiene / Management

Dirty data is the cause of many problems in marketing and business. Dirty data plays an especially harsh role in email marketing and deliverability.

What can you do to improve your data hygiene?

The first step in good data is in the collection. Start with clean data. Sounds easy, but it's not. Any time someone adds anything to your database, your goal is to get it right. Human error and judgement play a role in this.

One way to get it right is by standardizing your data. By adding a dropdown menu for fields, you can assure your data is standardized. For example, if you have country as a field, you are better off using a dropdown menu. That way you won't have "US, USA, U.S.A., United States, United States of America" for your country. You can standardize it to USA.

Secondly, you should be cleaning your data on a regular basis. For example, let's say you didn't have the above drop-down menu in place (maybe you didn't think about it before or maybe your CRM system doesn't allow it). You should set up a weekly or monthly program that changes all variations of United States to USA. You should be able to automate most of it (although you will probably still have to go through it because of misspellings and other entries that you may not have thought about).

Next, you should use some type of email validation tool. One example of a data validation tool is BriteVerify. There are many on the market, so figure out which one is best for your CRM, email service provider and/or your marketing automation tool. This tool validates the email address. This significantly cuts down on email bounces.

Why is it important to cut down on email bounces?

Your email service provider looks at that type of data to determine if your data and database is 'good' and can be trusted. By having a low bounce rate, your email deliverability goes up. This shows your ESP that you are trustworthy.
In addition to using a tool like BriteVerify, you will also want to run queries on your email service provider, CRM or marketing automation tool to remove people that have bounced a certain number of times over a specified period. An example would be anyone that has soft bounced 3 times within the last 6 months

unces (emails that are no longer valid --- company, the email address changed, ioved right away.

ssage relevant is good for marketing and business. .. io good for deliverability (and hopefully they all work together).

You need to segment your database. How is this related to keeping it relevant? By segmenting, you can split people by demographics as well as interests. This allows you to send a different message to women looking for hair highlights and men who are interested in a fancy barber shave.

Segmenting your list is about putting certain types of people in different 'segments. You may categorize people by demographics (male/female, age, etc.), psychographics (interests, personality, lifestyle) or geographic (location). Once you have your list segmented, make sure you make the message resonate with that group. You can do this by knowing what questions they have, their concerns, and what keeps them up at night. The more relevant your message, the more likely people will engage with your email.

Keep It Consistent

Consistency is important in emails on several levels. First, your name, email, subject line, and preheader should match your email body and call to action. Clickbait may get you some opens in the beginning, but it will quickly make your list not trust you. Once you lose the trust, you lose engagement, and your deliverability goes into the toilet.

Consistently send emails. If you send an email once every 7 months, it's hard to build a following and it's hard to have people remember you. Be consistent with your emails. Make sure your emails are sent often enough for people to remember you (but not too often to be burdensome).

Using triggered campaigns allows you to trigger email sends when a user or prospect engages or performs some type of action.

Keep Engagement Up

Keeping it relevant and keeping it consistent helps you keep engagement up.

Keeping a clean list is also key to engagement.
One thing many email professionals talk about is "cleaning your IP address." Sounds weird? Well, it's simpler than it sounds.

The best way to clean your IP address is to send to engaged users. It all goes back to the trust your ESP has for your data and the trust other servers have for you and your ESP. So, if tons of people on your list are opening and clicking on the links, servers assume it's a good email (and will continue to send emails to the inbox). If you are sending lots of bounces or emails that no one opens or clicks on, servers start to assume your email is junk (and they deposit it right into the junk folder or prevent it from even entering the server).

Check for the Bad Stuff
Check for spam traps. Spam traps are often created by mailbox providers. They are emails that are often acquired by bots 'scraping' websites for emails.

Check blacklists. Internet Service providers often create a database of identified IP addresses and /or domains that are known to send spam.

Keep spam low by following good email rules. Practice good email etiquette like using opt in email addresses, include easy-to-find unsubscribe links, and keep your list clean.

Don't Be Afraid to Delete
We talked about keeping your data clean earlier. But it's important that you are not afraid of deleting bad data and deleting unengaged contacts.

If you do this regularly, your database will be more effective and more engaged. In the email world (especially in the email service provider world), ratios matter. Make sure your ratio of engaged users compared to your overall database is high.

Tackle the Technical

Tell the ISP where you are sending from. You do this by authenticating your email. This will help the ISP know that you can be trusted.

1. SPF (Sender Policy Framework) - Sender Policy Framework is an email authentication method designed to detect forging sender addresses during the delivery of the email.
    For more information on creating an SPF record, check out Google's instructions here.
    https://support.google.com/a/answer/33786?hl=en&visit_id=1-636673658331759912-3236752279&rd=1
2. DKIM (DomainKeys Identified Mail) – DKIM is a technical standard that helps protect email senders and recipients from spam, spoofing, and phishing. It is a form of email authentication that allows an organization to claim responsibility for a message in a way that can be validated by the recipient. Here's how to authenticate email with DKIM here
    https://support.google.com/a/answer/174124?hl=en
3. DMARC (Domain-based Message Authentication, Reporting and Conformance) - DMARC is an email authentication protocol. It is designed to give email domain owners the ability to protect their domain from unauthorized use, commonly known as email spoofing. Here's how to add your DMARC record:
    https://support.google.com/a/answer/2466563?hl=en

You should work with your IT department or your Email Service Provider to ensure that you have taken care of all of these.

You can't have a great ROI if you can't get in the inbox.

XI. Get Your Emails Opened

Now that you know how to get your emails into the inbox, it's time to get them opened.

Subject Line

When it comes to getting emails opened, the subject line is usually the best place to start. Your subject line should give the email recipient a taste of what is to come.

A few best practices are below. Keep in mind that best practices are a great place to start. But you should be testing your database to see what works best. Most ESPs (email service providers) make it very easy to test the subject line.

1. Personalize – Include the contact's name or company name in the subject. I've tested this again and again, and it always holds true.
2. Ask a question – Asking questions prompts people to want to answer. Make sure the question is relevant to the email body. You can add 1 and 2 together. Example: "Robyn, do you think email is dead?"
3. Use numbers – Using numbers or percentages draws people in. Example: 7 Ways to Get People to Open Your Email
4. Use title case – Using Title Case (see what I did there?) is effective. What is title case? It's capitalizing every main word like you would do in a book title. This is a best practice. And personally, I've tested this in several databases.

Preview Text

What is the preview text? It's the text that is right under the subject line in the inbox. Most people let this default to the first few words listed in the email. Don't do this. This is valuable real estate you will want to use.

Use the best practices above (from subject lines) for preview text. You will want to personalize it. Use preview text as a great teaser.

From Email / Email Address

Most of the time you will want to use someone's name vs. a company or department. For example, I will use Robyn | robyn@robynhatfield.com instead of Sales | sales@robynhatfield.com.

I would suggest testing this. I have had mixed results on this one. Sometimes the name works better and sometimes the company information works better.

If your company is well known and has goodwill, you may want to try adding the company name with the first name. Example: Jane, Tesla Motors | jane@teslamotors.com.

Date and Time of Send

Statistically, Tuesday and Thursdays are best, and mornings are typically better. But this differs SIGNIFICANTLY across industry, title, demographics, etc. I've tested this with high-end engineers who performed better after 3pm on Tuesday, Wednesday and Thursday. I've tested it with C level executives that typically performed better before 7:30am and after 5:30pm on Tuesday, Wednesday, or Thursday. As with everything, make sure you test for your database.

Frequency

How often should you send emails? That's an impossible question. But if you do too much or too little, your engagement will fall. I suggest starting with weekly and keeping track of the metrics (both opens and clicks). Adjust accordingly.

List

Your list is EVERYTHING. Make sure it's clean and is the right target market. If you're not sure what I mean by clean, check out earlier chapters on list and data hygiene.

All the above are suggestions and best practices. However, you must TEST every assumption and suggestion. Test every component. The best way to do this is to test only one thing at a time (so you can have a 'control' email and a 'test' email). You can do AB split testing or ABCDEFG testing (as long as you are holding everything constant in one email and the differences in the other email or emails is just one variable).

Fun Stuff for Testing

We love testing subject lines and we love tools to help us. Check out some awesome subject lines here: http://robynhatifeld.com/email-resources

Ready to optimize your subject line? Try these tools: Below are websites that will grade your subject line on a variety of criteria. Each one provides something that's a little different, so it may make sense to check out all of them.

- Email Subject Line Grader
  >> http://emailsubjectlinegrader.com/
- Coschedule >> https://coschedule.com/headline-analyzer
- Subject Line.com >> https://www.subjectline.com/

APPEARANCE OF YOUR SUBJECT LINE
Do you want to know how your email will appear on different mobile devices? This website shows you how your name, email address, subject and pretext will appear on iPhones, Androids, etc.

Zurb >> https://zurb.com/playground/testsubject

READABILITY
How easy is your subject line or copy to read? Ideally, you are going for a grade 9.
Hemingway App >> http://www.hemingwayapp.com/

SPAM CHECKER
This website will check to see if your email will trigger a SPAM filter. When you go to the site, it shows you an email address for you to send your email to.
Is Not Spam >> http://www.isnotspam.com/

These tools will help you improve your email subject lines and email copy. HOWEVER, the most important thing you can do to improve your email is ALWAYS to TEST, TEST, TEST! :)

Again, you can access all of the above resources at
http://robynhatifeld.com/email-resources

By optimizing your open rate, you increase your ability to get conversions.

Don't forget...

More conversions = Better ROI

XII. Get the Clicks

You've delivered your email into the inbox. You have optimized every part of your email to get it opened.

Now you need to focus on getting the recipient to click your CTA.

So, what's a CTA? It's a call to action! It's the thing you want the email recipient to do (and the main reason why you are sending the email).

Calls to action can be visiting a blog, watching a video, registering for an event or webinar, downloading an eBook or whitepaper, and so much more.

A lot of the things that you've done so far to get the email into the inbox and get it opened also help with getting clicks.

List
The right list is key. When you deliver the right message to the right people, they take action. Don't send an email to your entire list. Make sure you segment your list as much as possible and as much as makes sense.

If your product is different for men and women, separate them. If your product or service is specific to an industry, make sure to focus on that industry. If your decision maker is a Director and above, remove anyone else that isn't director for this email send.

Even if you have an engaged, clean list, you still need to segment. This allows you to deliver a tailored message (and makes your email something that people look forward to).

Messaging
Is the messaging right for this specific audience? That's the question you should ask EVERY time BEFORE sending any email.

Does your audience care about what you are talking about? If it's just a bunch of babble about your company, don't bother. It should be solving one of THEIR problems, answering one of THEIR questions, alleviating one of THEIR concerns. If it doesn't do this, start over!

Also, are the words and phrases you are using what your target audience uses? Use the common phrases and words of your industry. This not only tells your audience you understand them, it tells them that you are on their same team.

Offer
Is your offer something that your list wants? Even if the offer is just directing them to a blog post, does it answer a question or solve a problem they have?

Call to Action
Is the call to action clear? It better be! Because one of the worst things to do is make it confusing.

Create a clear and concise call to action. Stick to only 1 per email (there are exceptions to this --- but keep this as a rule).

Below are some best practices when it comes to calls to action:

- Use buttons – Buttons typically perform better than links.
- Repeat the same CTA – Use only 1 CTA but repeat it throughout the email.
- Insert a call-to-action button in the header of the email (so they see it when they open the email).
- Include a link in the body of the email.
- Add a button at the bottom of the email.
- Test the color of the button. Typically, red performs better for me. But test the color of the email. It's important to test only one thing at a time. So have a control email and then test all different color buttons.
- Use short, action-oriented language in the button. And test that button. Example: Download the White Paper, Download the eBook, Watch This Video, Register Today.
- Use UTM parameters to see where people click. For example, if you have the same CTA several times in the email, you will want to know which button or link they clicked. This can be done by adding:
  - ?top
  - ?middle-link
  - ?bottom
  - or some other variance. See UTM parameters below for more information.

UTM Parameters

UTM parameters should be used in all areas of your marketing. UTM, which stands for Urchin Tracking Module, is a simple code that is attached to the end of a URL that passes data to Google Analytics for digital campaigns.

Think of it as a magic tracking function.

Why are UTM parameters included in this section? Because you need to know what campaigns are working. The best way to know is to look at the clicks on CTAs in emails and then what subsequent actions they take on the website. You do that by using UTM parameters!

You can set up the UTM parameter so you can identify what the source, campaign, content, etc. is. I have a link to a Google Analytics UTM builder here: http://robynhatfield.com/email-resources.

UTMs are a very valuable tracking tool to help you make better decisions. A few important points to remember are:
- Be consistent
- Use dashes
- Don't repeat yourself
- Use lower case
- Keep it simple but descriptive.

Use UTMs consistently so you will have enough data from many sources to make good decisions. You also want to be consistent with your naming convention.

Make sure you don't repeat a name. This will ensure you have only one traffic source for each UTM.

Use lower case instead of camel case to prevent human error. It's easy to forget if you capitalized something. If you keep it lower case, it just keeps it simple.

For UTMs make sure you keep it simple but be descriptive. You will want the name to tell you right away where that traffic is coming from.

UTMs should be used across your marketing efforts. Below are 3 examples of ways you can use UTMs:

1. Insert UTM parameters in the URLs you share on your social media profiles.
   This is a great way to differentiate all the different links on your social media. You should use different UTMs for your profile link, post links, comment links, and promoted content.
2. Test the clicks from different email newsletters.
   Use different UTMs in different emails.
3. Track the characteristics of the most effective banner advertisements. UTMs allow you to quickly see what is working and what is not.

UTMs allow you to track data across different media as well as track certain campaigns. If you have a certain type of content you share across different media, you may use the campaign term to track what is gaining traction across all platforms.

Here's how it works. You answer the following questions (the first 4 are required, the last 2 are optional):
    1. Website URL*
    2. Campaign Source*
    3. Campaign Medium*
    4. Campaign Name*
    5. Campaign Term
    6. Campaign Content

Campaign Source utm_source	Required. Use utm_source to identify a search engine, newsletter name, or other source. Example: google
Campaign Medium utm_medium	Required. Use utm_medium to identify a medium such as email or cost-per-click. Example: cpc
Campaign Name utm_campaign	Required. Used for keyword analysis. Use utm_campaign to identify a specific product promotion or strategic campaign. Example: utm_campaign=spring_sale
Campaign Term utm_term	Used for paid search. Use utm_term to note the keywords for this ad. Example: running+shoes
Campaign Content utm_content	Used for A/B testing and content-targeted ads. Use utm_content to differentiate ads or links that point to the same URL. Examples: logolink or textlink

So, if I answered the above with:

1. http://robynhatfield.com
2. internal
3. email
4. spring-2021
5. sweaters
6. Texas

Here's a screenshot of the Google Analytics Builder:

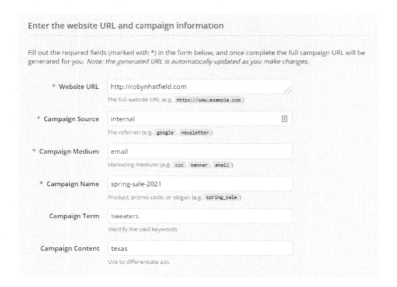

Then the code I am copying is:
http://robynhatfield.com/?utm_source=internal&utm_medium=email&utm_campaign=spring-sale-2021&utm_term=sweaters&utm_content=texas

Design and Formatting

The look and feel of the email is important to people reading and clicking on your content. We talked about clean HTML code for your email to be delivered (email servers often look at the HTML code to see if the HTML follows the latest standards).

In addition, your email should look clean and should be easy to read. The actions you want the recipient to take should be very clear.

If you use images, you should use relevant, high-resolution, eye-popping images that help tell the story you want to tell.

I suggest adding links to all images. When people click on an image, they are redirected to your desired location.

Other Stuff

As we mentioned in the beginning of this chapter, many of the actions you've taken to getyour email in the inbox and opened also apply here. You should be testing what day and time is best for your list. You should test the frequency. And you should double check all areas of the 'how to get opens' chapter.

> **Getting the clicks is one step closer to getting the conversions!**
>
> **Think of doing each step better and you'll skyrocket your ROI!**

XIII. Get Conversions

Most website conversions are out of scope for this book. However, it's important to understand conversions as it pertains to email marketing.

If you can, try to get some type of ownership of the metrics (for example – getting access to Google Analytics) so you can always test and analyze the data.

If you own the website (i.e., you're the business owner vs. being in digital marketing for a company), you should have some type of analytics tracker on your website. Google Analytics is great because it's free.

Here's more information on how to set up Google Analytics on your site:
https://support.google.com/analytics/answer/1008015

Calls to action within emails should be clear. The same applies to calls to actions on the website and landing pages. Don't send someone to the home page of your website. They won't know what to do. Bring people to a page that has a clear path and a clear action that should be taken.

If you are pushing someone to a video on your page or a blog, you may want to add some type of call to action at the bottom of the page. Once they read the blog, is there a next step they should do? Maybe read another blog? Or read a white paper or eBook that goes into more detail about the topic you covered in the blog? Think about what journey you want people to go on once they take the first action.

If you are sending someone to a video, make sure the video is at the top (or easy to get to when they get to the page).

If you have gated content (content that requires you to complete a form), landing pages are great for this.

Remember: The landing page needs to deliver on the promise you made in the email. If you say 7 Ways to Get Past the Gatekeeper, your landing page should use that same title (and if images were used, you should use the same or similar images on the page).

You want congruence between all parts of your email as well as the landing page or web page that the CTA points to.

Just like the email, you should be testing every part of the landing page including the header and/or title, the body, the images/videos, the form, the call to action, etc.

Best Ways to Optimize Conversions on Your Page

1. Test all parts of the page. Do A/B split tests on each part just like you did for emails. Consider using Google Optimize. Click here for more information on Optimize.
2. Remove distractions. If you can make this page as clean as possible with an obvious next step, your conversions will improve.
3. For the form, decrease the amount of information required. Can you start with name and email address? The more fields you have (and the more you ask for), the lower the completion rate. You may consider using progressive forms. This allows you to ask for a few pieces of information each time. For example, the first

time you come to my site, I ask your name and email. When you come again (and my site recognizes you by IP address), I ask you to fill in phone number and state. The next time, I may ask for your mailing address.

4. Test pop ups. If you are sending people to a blog or other non-gated form, you may want to try using pop ups. These are forms that 'pop up' when a person is on a website for a certain amount of time or when the person clicks on certain things.

5. Try to offer something better. This is obvious, but worth stating. If you're not getting conversions, you may consider offering something else…something better. If you have a checklist, maybe you make it a bundle of a checklist, reference guide, and how-to video. Test what works, but make it irresistible!

6. Address the normal objections people have for giving their information. If you do this upfront, you should see increases in conversion.

7. Use testimonials. Social proof is golden. Use testimonials to help build trust and credibility.

8. Make it easy to convert. Make it easy to find the form or field. Make it easy to complete. If you can, allow your form to autofill from a social media platform or from Google.

9. Create a full program on the back end to follow up with the person (once they put in their information, BAMMMMM, we are in email marketing funnel heaven).

Conversions are GLORIOUS gold for your ROI!

XIV. What to Measure

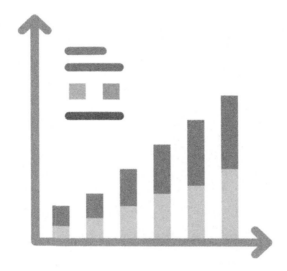

When it comes to email marketing, what you measure really depends on your goals.

I've heard people say, "I know it's working because I'm getting clients."

True, but you're really missing the boat.

You want to optimize every part of the marketing process. If you do this, you will significantly increase your client acquisition.

Let's say you decide to try to increase each part of your email marketing by 10%.

Starting Numbers:
Email Sends: 100,000
Delivered (90%): 90,000
Opened (20%): 18,000
Clicked (5%): 900
Converted (1%): 9

Improve Each by 10%:
Email Sends: 100,000
Delivered (99%): 99,000
Opened (22%): 21,780
Clicked (5.5%): 1197.90
Converted (1.1%): 13.17

That is a 46.33% increase in overall conversion!

If all you were measuring was overall client acquisition, you may just focus on the conversion rate. That would have increased to 1.1% on the original clicked of 900. So instead of 13+ customers, you have 9.9 customers.

Imagine if this was a daily number you were running. Over the course of the year, the difference would be: 3,292.50 clients (13.17 x 250) vs. 2,475. If your product is $200, the difference in revenue is:
$163,500 ($658,500 - $495,000).

That's why you TEST & OPTIMIZE EVERY PART!

Now that I've (hopefully) drilled that in, below is a list of metrics and the definition:

1. Deliverability Rate –Total number of delivered emails divided by the number of emails sent. We want as close to 100% as possible.
2. Open Rate – Total number of unique opens divided by the total number of delivered emails.
3. Click Rate or Click Through Rate – Total number of unique clicks divided by the total number of delivered emails.
4. Click to Open Rate – Total number of unique clicks divided by the total number of unique opens.
5. Conversion Rate – Total number of conversions on a web page divided by the total number of visitors.
6. Unsubscribe Rate – Total number of unsubscribes divided by the total number of delivered emails.
7. Bounce Rate – Total number of email bounces divided by the total number of delivered emails.

8. Complaints – Total number of complaints
9. List growth rate - % the list grows over a specified period of time.
10. Overall ROI – The total amount of revenue generated over the cost.

Key Point: Many of the above are great if you are looking at email marketing in a vacuum.

If you do a good job of attribution (process of matching customer sales to specific marketing activities to understand where revenue is coming from and optimize marketing spend in the future), you can focus on client acquisition and revenue generation.

Because, after all, that's what we want. More clients and more money! ⍰

> **Now you know the secret to Email ROI.**
>
> **Optimize and maximize EVERY part of the process.**

XV. Conclusion

Email marketing is amazingggg. Email marketing is effective. Email marketing works.

Really, do you need more than that? ▨

I hope this book provided you with tips, techniques, strategies, and resources that will help you on your email marketing journey.

If you loved this book, please send me an email at robyn@robynhatfield.com. If you want to share it via social media, please use the hashtag #roifocusedemailguide so I can make sure to follow along.

Oh yeah…and definitely check out the next chapter. It's one of my favorites because I was able to talk to some amazing email marketing professionals and grabbed tips from each of them.

XVI. Tips from Email Marketing Professionals

Like many areas of marketing and sales, email marketing has experts with all different views.

Why? We have all had different successes and failures. We've worked with different databases, target markets, and segmentations.

We've all had different experiences.

One of the beautiful things about networking is being able to call on the expertise of your network.

I reached out to fellow email marketing and marketing operations professionals and asked if they would share some of their expertise and knowledge in email marketing.

I hope you enjoy and get as much out of their tips as I did!

The Experts

Above all else, be ruthlessly honest with yourself about how well you know and understand your audience. Every touchpoint should directly add value to the recipient. Like every other marketing activity, this will require a deep understanding of your audience. Everything else builds from that understanding, so you can't skip that step. Without it you can miss the mark on who needs your content (targeting), what your audience actually needs (value), and how they want to consume it (copy/design).

Chris Glanzman
Director of Product Marketing

Audience segmentation is the most important aspect of email marketing. Ensuring that your messaging is being received by contacts who will find that specific message relevant, beneficial, and interesting is key to successful email marketing campaigns. It will impact everything from open and click through rates to conversion and nurture rates.

Kevin Johnson
Email Marketing

An underrated skill in email marketing is the ability to identify risk early. Whether you're building a simple newsletter or highly complex automations, there is plenty to go wrong.

For example, in a simple newsletter there could be an incorrect or broken link, a typo in the body or subject line, too large image files, forgetting pre-header text, not segmenting like you could be, not adequately suppressing users who aren't engaged, etc.

When building automations or triggered emails, there are more structural nuances such as measuring how a certain flow will impact other flows, ensuring you're not over-emailing, making sure there's sound personalization, checking if/then statements in conditional logic, adequately setting re-entry wait time periods for the user to fire the trigger again, and much more.

Seeing what can potentially go wrong for your email program is what I encourage folks to do before, during, and after any project. If you, as an email marketer, can identify and diagnose what can go wrong early, that preparedness not only will help you succeed in your career but also create better experiences for your subscribers.

Joel Debus
Email Marketing Manager at Knowledge to Practice

In my opinion, one KPI that's often given too much weight when determining the success (or failure) of an email campaign is the open rate - especially if you're focusing mostly on B2B marketing.

The reason I say this is because there are some desktop email clients such as Outlook that don't display images by default the way most web-based clients do. And some ESPs like Pardot will only register an open if a tiny 1x1 tracking pixel is fired. If the images aren't enabled or displayed (especially if you're sending a text-heavy email, and recipients don't feel that they have to enable images), then the 1x1 tracking pixel won't fire, and the email won't register as being opened.

I performed an experiment a few years back to test this behavior. I personally asked 20 of my co-workers to open an email I sent to them from Pardot, without performing any other action. I didn't tell them what the test was for so I could see who naturally enabled their images from within their desktop client or checked the email on the web. All 20 recipients opened the email through some version of Outlook and reported back to me that they opened the email and nothing else. I even spoke to each recipient individually and in person just to make sure they opened it.

In theory, Pardot should have reported a 100% open rate. However, the actual data that came back reported a 65% open rate, which would mean only 13 people opened the email. I knew for a fact that all 20 of my co-workers opened the email, so this test was very telling.

Because of this test, I started measuring success based on other data such as clickthrough rates, the average time spent on the website, pages per session when a visitor came from email, bounce rate, unsubscribes, and, of course, market feedback to see if we were sending emails too frequently (or not enough).

Brian Choongphol
Marketing Automation Manager

Email Marketing is extremely important when it comes to your business or nonprofit organization. You're probably thinking, what will you share and how will you begin.

It's really simple, trust me.

If you don't know where to start, simply introduce yourself and offer a quick download of a checklist, list of tips and tricks that can help your audience, or a video/webinar of you solving a problem that they may have. Once you have your first email sent, begin working on your future content that will add value to your audience. Think about questions your clients often ask you, you can turn that into an email marketing campaign. If that doesn't work for you, you can always turn a social media or blog post into an email marketing campaign.

Your email list belongs to you, unlike your website or social media (after all, you're just renting a tiny space on the internet). You are able to craft your email exactly how you want it and add the most value to it for your people.

Think about it...

You're creating a message that must have a call to action, if it doesn't, the entire email is pointless. When it comes to email marketing, you MUST add value. No matter how many emails you send, if there isn't any value, the person on the other side of the computer (or smartphone) doesn't entertain the email. So, if you spend hours on one email marketing campaign yourself, you've honestly wasted your time. If you've done this already, it may be time to outsource it, so you're able to shift your focus back on your business or nonprofit.

Remember, always add value and a call to action to your content. People want to know that you have the answer to their problem and you're going to help them solve it.

Haeshah Z. Davis
Founder of HZD Creates

I tell my colleagues all the time that one of the most important strategies for marketers to use is email personalization. Personalization goes further than just including a person's name in your email. It's important to analyze your data to pull in intricate details about each of your subscribers to deliver information they care about. A great example of this is when companies provide product suggestions based on previous purchases or order history!

Kelsey Shirley
Email Marketing Manager

APPENDIX 1
Definitions

Email marketing has its own lingo. You have probably heard many of these terms, but you may not know exactly what they mean.

Bounce Rate

The rate at which your emails are not delivered. An acceptable bounce rate is less than 5%. Soft bounce is when you have a temporary issue the email wasn't delivered. A hard bounce is when the email is no longer valid.

CAN-SPAM

Short for 'Controlling the Assault of Non-Solicited Pornography And Marketing Act of 2003.' CAN-SPAM outlines rules for commercial email, establishes requirements, provides email recipients an out or way to unsubscribe, and defines the consequences for violations of the Act.

CTR (Click-Through Rate)

The percentage of clicks within the email (click on a URL within the email). This is shown as a percentage of people that the email is delivered to.

CTO (Click to Open)

The percentage of clicks within the email (click on a URL within the email) as a percentage of emails opened.

Conversion Rate

This is also shown as a percentage. It shows the percent of people that responded to the call to action (rather than just any click).

Double Opt-In

Double opt-in requires subscribers to request to be added to the list and then confirm again. While this is the best way to prevent complaints, it also results in the lowest amount of opt ins. Some marketers choose this while others don't for the obvious benefits and problems.

House List (or Prospect/Customer List)
This is gold. This is a list that is permission-based that you built yourself with opt-in subscribers.

HTML vs. Plain Text Email
The pretty emails you see are HTML. You can use HTML to design the emails. There is also plain text which is text only. Most email software programs allow you to create both, so you give your email recipients the option to choose.

List Segmentation
When you segment your list, you are putting your email subscribers into different categories depending on a variety of different things such as client vs. prospect, age, sex, preferences, etc. The more you can segment your list, the better you will be able to target the information (and have more people engaged with the content included in your email).

Open Rate
This is the percentage of emails that were opened in a campaign.

Opt In / Opt Out
Opt in means someone subscribed to be on your email list. Opt out means someone unsubscribed (and no longer wants to receive your emails).

Triggered Automation

This allows you to send different emails depending on what action the email recipient takes. For example, if someone does not open an email, they may receive the same email a 2nd time. If they open it, they may receive one email. And if they open it and click on a link inside the email, they get a different email. This allows you to really target your list and be able to see who is most interested in the topic.

APPENDIX 2
Real Life Examples

Soul Cycle

If you don't know what Soul Cycle is, it's a fitness company that sells spin cycle classes. Soul Cycle is very expensive compared to other classes. They are all about the experience!

I went to a Soul Cycle class with a friend (who loves SC). When it comes to onboarding and getting people back, they are amazing!

How It Started:

A friend suggested I come to a Soul Cycle class. She pointed me to the website. The customer experience began with this easy-to-navigate and easy-to-use website. I was able to create an account, buy a class and book my bike in advance quickly and easily. They minimized friction at every point.

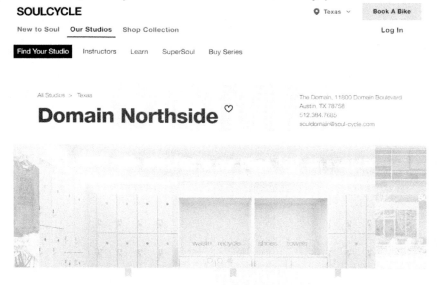

Soul Cycle then sends me onboarding emails that explain what the process will be and what I need to bring.

It starts with the welcome (after you create your account):

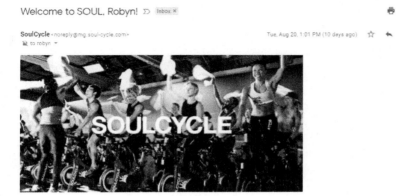

Then after you purchase, you get your receipt. Note the look and feel of the email.

SOULCYCLE

Purchaser Receipt

Order # 32319141

Purchaser: Robyn Hatfield

Order Date: Aug 20, 2019

Order Location: Web Store

Order Items

Style	Size	Qty	Price	Extended
SERIESFIRSTTIMERIDE-FL-TX-MA-SOCAL expires in 30 days	1	1	$ 20.00	$ 20.00
		Subtotal		$ 20.00
		Shipping		$ 0.00
		Taxes		$ 0.00

Then you are notified that you're in (i.e. you have a bike reserved). In the email, it says to let the front desk know you're new so they can help you find and set up your bike.

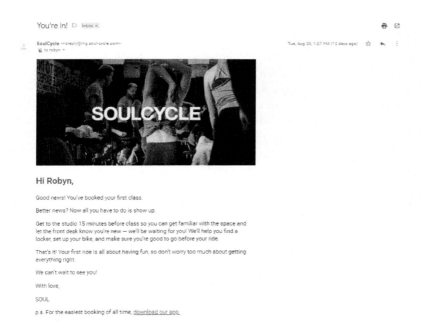

The next email tells you your first ride is tomorrow.

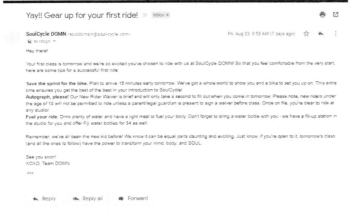

Knowing that starting something new can be nerve-wracking, Soul Cycle gives you the low-down on some things to remember. They decrease buyer's remorse and encourage participation by reminding you how great the instructor is and how fun the vibe will be.

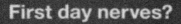

First day nerves?
Don't sweat it!
Save that for class.

Come to the studio 15 minutes early
and our staff will take care of the rest.

The Workout
High-intensity cardio
Strength training
Rhythm-based choreography

The Instructor
Radiates magnetic energy
Creates killer playlists
Inspires you to be your best self

The Vibe
Intimate, candlelit studio
Movement synced to the music
A community riding as one

And, did we mention it's SO fun?
You're going to do great.

LET'S DO THIS

When you arrive, you have people all around. You check-in at the front desk. If you are a newbie (like I was), they have you marked. They give special attention to first timers. I had a locker with my name on it. As soon as I changed into my shoes, someone was waiting to take me to my bike. They made sure I had the right weights, that my bike was exactly set for me (literally adjusted my bike for me).

After the class was over, they asked me how it went (no sales push or pressure — just a real question on how the ride went).

After I completed the class (which kicked my @ss), I received this email. It celebrates me and reinforces this behavior. I love the imagery and simple call to action.

SOULCYCLE

Your first ride is a big deal!

Think of this as a virtual high five from us. We know how tough it can be to try something new!

Let's keep riding!

BOOK A BIKE

What was class #1 like?

We want to hear everything. Head here and give us the details.

TAKE THE SURVEY

I then get an email for a special package price. Again, celebrating that I CRUSHED it (obviously they did not watch me in class).

SOULCYCLE

Now the real fun starts!
Meet the Starter Pack.

**Three classes.
Triple the fun.
At a special price —
just for you!***

*Offer only available before booking your second ride.

For Labor Day, I received another email for package pricing.

SOULCYCLE

From us, to you.

Start the season with a 5-pack— at a special price.

Dedicated riders like you make our Soul community one-of-a-kind. So as a little thank you, we're helping you jump-start the new season with a specially-priced pack.

Just apply code **LABORDAY20** at checkout—and ride straight into fall on the bike next to us.

GET YOUR PACK

All the emails incorporate their fresh, clean, energetic and happy brand. All the emails have simple calls to action. Soul Cycle has a beautiful online and offline customer experience. Other brands…take note!

Marketing Profs

If you are in marketing, Marketing Profs always provides tons of great information. Not only do they have consistently great information, but they follow a beautifully clean layout.
The below image is a great example.

If you notice, they have 1 call to action for the email but it is repeated. They show it at the top, in the body (with a link), then again at the bottom.

Using videos in emails often increases overall click through rates and engagement.

If you're looking to create more awareness and demand for your products, you won't want to miss our next B2B Backstage event happening February 9. But don't take our word for it: hear from our keynote speaker, best-selling author and world-famous marketer, Andrew Davis:

Get your Backstage Pass to see Andrew by becoming a PRO member today.

I WANT TO SEE ANDREW

With your PRO membership, you'll also get access to B2B Forum Online (April and October), Master Classes, Bootcamps, courses, and a lively Facebook group.

Constant Contact

Constant Contact is an email service provider. They have ramped up their offering in the last few years.

Even if you are not in the market, you've probably heard of them. They advertise on TV and online and have a great affiliate network.

While I'm personally not a big fan of newsletters, I think Constant Contact does a great job at nailing their target market. While I don't think they used much in personalization, I do think they are absolutely aligned with the pains, concerns, and questions of their target market (small business).

They start with the image sizes of social media. If you're like me, it's something you look up all the time.

In the email, it also has a webinar. It's great to add in a high commitment link. This allows you to pull people through the buyer's journey.

The email ends with explaining a relatively new feature, a quick tip, and a list of blogs.

Hey hi hello!

I'm excited to share that this edition of *Hints & Tips* features our 2021 Social Media Image Sizes Cheat Sheet, something near and dear to my heart as the manager of our social media accounts here at Constant Contact! You're going to want to bookmark this one and keep it close for when you're creating new graphics or images to share online. We're also diving in on other ways to keep your social media on the right track this year.

Let's get this show on the road!

Ashley Perssico
Marketing Manager, Social Media

P.S. Don't forget to follow us on social media for marketing advice, stories from small businesses just like yours, and so much more.

Social Media Image Sizes Cheat Sheet

It's clear that you shouldn't ignore the power of visuals when it comes to social media marketing. However, it's a challenge to keep up with the ever-changing image size guidelines for social media. The impact of posting visuals goes down when you post one that is awkwardly cropped or can't be viewed on certain devices, so it's important to get it right.

That's why we've created this social media image size guide for Facebook, Instagram, Pinterest, Twitter, YouTube, and LinkedIn.

Get the guide

FREE WEBINAR

Making Sense of Online Marketing for Technology Service Providers

With a wave of technology platforms and tools sweeping overall business industries, the Technology Services industry is being looked to as a leading source of knowledge and assistance for using said platforms for small business clients. Does your agency stand out as a leading expert?

Whether you're just getting started with online marketing or not seeing the results you've hoped for then this session is for you. With our guest expert, Liz Harr of Hinge Marketing, you'll learn a smarter, more practical approach to building awareness around your business. From differentiating your agency through organic searches to building off of clients' referrals, showcasing your expertise and more - find out how to get the word out to the people who need your help the most, online.

You'll learn:

- How people find you online with organic and paid search tools
- How to set yourself up for success through various digital marketing channels
- How it all comes together as a digital marketing strategy

NOTE: If you are unable to attend, please register anyway. We'll send you a free recording of the webinar which you can watch on your own time.

Thur, Jan 28, 2021, 2:00 PM - 3:00 PM ET

Register now

Create and Schedule Social Posts in Constant Contact

Connect your Facebook and Instagram accounts, Twitter account, or LinkedIn account and start creating and sharing posts;

Check to see how it's performing and respond to any comments all from within your Constant Contact account!

Check it out

QUICK TIP

Create a Poll

Wondering what your followers want to see from you on your social media platforms? Just ask them! Facebook, Twitter, Instagram Stories, and even LinkedIn allow you to create a poll to gauge what your supporters would like to see more of.

Read the latest from the blog

2021 Online Marketing Calendar: Free Template and Full List of Holidays
A little bit of planning goes a long way when it comes to marketing your business or organization online. But we know it can [...]

Watch: Last-Minute Holiday Marketing Ideas to Drive More Retail Sales
The busy holiday shopping season is upon us. At Constant Contact, we know the majority of small businesses start their [...]

15 Last-Minute Holiday Email Marketing Ideas

Warby Parker

Oh Warby…how you WOO me! I've purchased 2 times from Warby Parker. One was a home try on and one was in store. I've recently gone back online to check out some glasses. The email they sent shows the exact glasses that I looked at (and hovered on) for days.
Take my money!

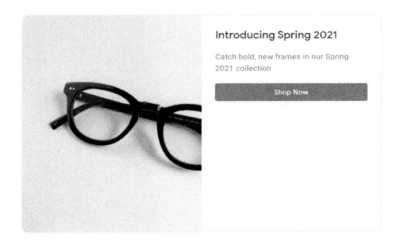

Fanatics

Fanatics does a great job at personalization. If you're a sports fan, you probably are familiar with Fanatics. It's great gear for all types of sports.

I have an account with Fanatics. I specified that my team is Texas A&M University. You see that's the first team the email shows (this is towards the middle of the email – above it were links to Fanatics).

But you will also see that it's showing UCF. It's not one of my listed teams, but Fanatics knows that I have purchased quite a few UCF items in the past. There's a reason...I have several people in my life that are UCF fans or alumni.

PICKS FOR YOU ∨

Texas A&M Aggies adidas Ultraboost 1.0 DNA Running Shoe - Maroon/White

Texas A&M Aggies Fanatics Authentic Framed 15" x 17" Franchise Foundations Collage

Texas A&M Aggies Nike 2021 Orange Bowl Champions Locker Room T-Shirt - Black

UCF Knights Nike Big Logo Performance Long Sleeve T-Shirt - Black

UCF Knights Fanatics Branded Distressed Arch Over Logo Long Sleeve Hit T-Shirt - Black

UCF Knights Colosseum Adult Logo Face Covering 2-Pack

Shop Aggies

Add Your Teams

Add Your Teams

Earn 🅕 FanCash On Every Purchase!

Vince Reed

This guy is an awesome marketer. He is in the internet marketing and traffic space. He has great videos and lots of great freebies.

Vince uses video extremely well. In the email below he uses a few fun things to get clicks:

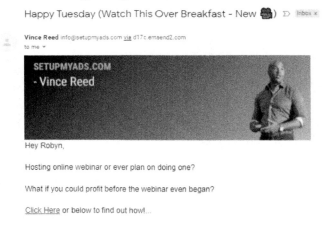

First, he uses an icon image in his subject line.

Secondly, he uses an image of himself in the header.

His emails are typically shorter. He uses a CTA link in the body as well as a video with a link (both the same link that brings you to a YouTube video).

Notice that his video image grabs your attention.
He uses a P.S. (which is surprisingly effective). In his P.S. he has the more direct CTA of setting an appointment (brings you to a calendar set up).

Neil Patel

Neil Patel is an SEO and lead generation expert. He built many freebie tools out there that generate leads for him daily. Two tools that I have personally used are Hello Bar and Ubersuggest.

Every email that I have receive from Neil (not saying every email he sends), is a simple text only email.
He has an image attached to his ID (so Gmail shows it to me).

Simple step-by-step instructions on how to get more traffic fast :) ⅀ inbox ×

Neil Patel <np@neilpatel.com>
to me ▾

What if there was a proven way to grow... to get more traffic...

Something that would take all the guesswork out of the equation?

As an entrepreneur, learning effective marketing strategies can be hard.

Which is why I am about to change that.

On February 23rd my team and I are going to break down how to do digital marketing, step-by-step, for any business.

Click here to sign up for free.

Cheers,

Neil Patel

Unsubscribe | Update your profile | 9718 River Trader St, Las Vegas, Nevada 89178

This email just has 1 CTA which is a link in the body.
For this email he is advertising his summit.
Neil is definitely someone I would suggest getting on his email list because he provides a ton of high value content, and he is a great marketer to learn from.

Sales Rebellion

The Sales Rebellion is a super cool community created by one of my favorite people to follow on LinkedIn, Dale Dupree.

This email is an email to help build a community. If you check out the link, it's a zoom link for their next meeting.

This company obviously does great marketing. My only changes would be I would:

1) Add a calendar invite so they could save it in their computer (so they get a reminder from their computer/phone).
2) I would add a link to the big image.

JLL

JLL is B2B gold in my opinion. They do an excellent job of segmenting their database automatically. Their content is very on point.

2nd February 2021

Trends & Insights

How cleaning the office is going the extra mile

Office refurbishments underway as landlords lure tenants

The evolution of malls? Signs emerge in China

Spotlight

PODCAST: When can fans expect the return of live sports?

Sports fans are ready to re-enter the arena to support their teams.

Read more

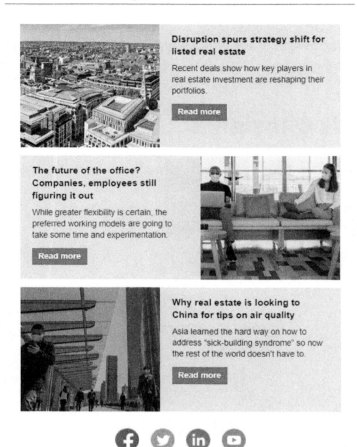

I received this email because I signed up for their general newsletter. They have a great, clean layout.

Based on your choices (where you go in the email and links), you will be segmented and will start to get more of the content you like.

Beautiful...just beautiful!

Salesforce

Salesforce is a major player in Customer Relationship Management (CRM) platforms. I currently use Salesforce every day. But recently I have been taking additional classes using their Trailhead platform (great training --- I would highly recommend it).

I logged onto Trailhead. Within a few minutes of logging off of Trailhead, I received this email. This is a personalized email. So this shows integrated alerts. I like the fact that they used my name in the preview text (the text right underneath the subject line). In the preview it also shows that they know that I was looking at stuff on Salesforce.

I think some people use this well and others don't. I loved this one. I sometimes get a little creeped out when people reply back (I see you were on our site). It's a thin line of responsive and helpful vs. creepy, stalker.

Salesforce nailed it in my opinion.

Example of Personalization

In this example, I wanted to point out a key thing to remember in personalization. If you add a token for personalization (for example, to include a name in an email), Typically your email service provider will add in the name exactly as it appears in the database or ESP (email service provider).

In the example below, it shows 2 different case styles. This is because I signed up for the email with 2 different email addresses (on accident). They both are sent to my one inbox. As you can see, one time I used ALL CAPS and one time I used capitalization.

This is important to remember because many people use all lower case when filling out forms. And it may look strange when you add it into the email.

You can fix this by either: 1) adding in script in your email program to always use capitalization (not all email service providers allow this), or 2) manually fix names or other fields you use on a regular basis.

bad news ROBYN - Bad news ROBYN: It WILL happen again. And when it does, it'll feel like the end of the world.

bad news Robyn - Bad news Robyn: It WILL happen again. And when it does, it'll feel like the end of the world. Es

APPENDIX 3
The Buyer's Journey in Detail

What is a Buyer's Journey and How Does It Relate to Email Marketing?

I added this to the appendix because it is so relevant but somewhat out of scope for this book.

A buyer's journey is the journey your prospect goes through before being a customer or before buying.

The best way to explain it is by giving an example of a buyer's journey that you have probably been a part of.

Let's say you have a car right now that meets your needs. It starts, it's relatively new (i.e., about 5 years old), and serves its purpose. You don't know you have a problem yet.

In the AWARENESS stage, we are trying to identify and point out the problem.

If we start communicating with you about a new Ford truck, you will dismiss us. Why? You have a car.

So, the AWARENESS stage is all about poking holes in assumptions and telling you about problems. We say "Most of the people we talk to have cars that are 5 years or older and are paid off. They originally felt that they didn't need a car. But once they started having car problems and repair costs, they knew it was time. Many of our customers said they wished they would have purchased a car sooner."

Again, we're trying to point out the problem. We are going to try to hit hot buttons that are common with people that have cars that are 5 years or older and are paid off.

We know that you will need a car soon. We want to be the first to bring you through the journey.

Once you say, "maybe I should start looking" that's the CONSIDERATION phase.

With the consideration stage, you are considering different solutions. Do you keep your car and pay the extra repairs? Do you buy a truck? Do you want to lease a car? You have unlimited options. But you are in the process of deciding.

How do you know if someone is in this phase? Great question! How smart is your marketing automation? If you have script on your website that talks to your marketing automation tool, you can see what pages people are going to. If you have a page that has a tool that lets you decide the cost of keeping a car vs. buying a new one, that's a great sign. If you have a page that talks about how to find the right vehicle for you, that's a great one. You can also send emails regarding these types of information and see who clicks on the links.

Let's say you have gone onto these sites, clicked some emails, etc. and we know that you are now past the consideration stage and moving into the DECISION stage.

You have made the decision to buy a full-size truck, but which truck and who will you buy it from?

The DECISION stage is about the buyer finding and buying the solution. If we are Chevy, we want to show you why a Chevy Silverado is better than a Ford F150, Toyota Tundra, etc. We are giving you detailed information on why we're better.

When you lay out the buyer's journey, you should create a series of emails that fall into each stage. Your goal, messaging, collateral, and collateral type should be different for each step.

Within the series, you keep a single focus. But each series should have a different focus.

Printed in Great Britain
by Amazon